COSMIC
CATASTROPHES
Seven Ways to Destroy a Planet Like Earth

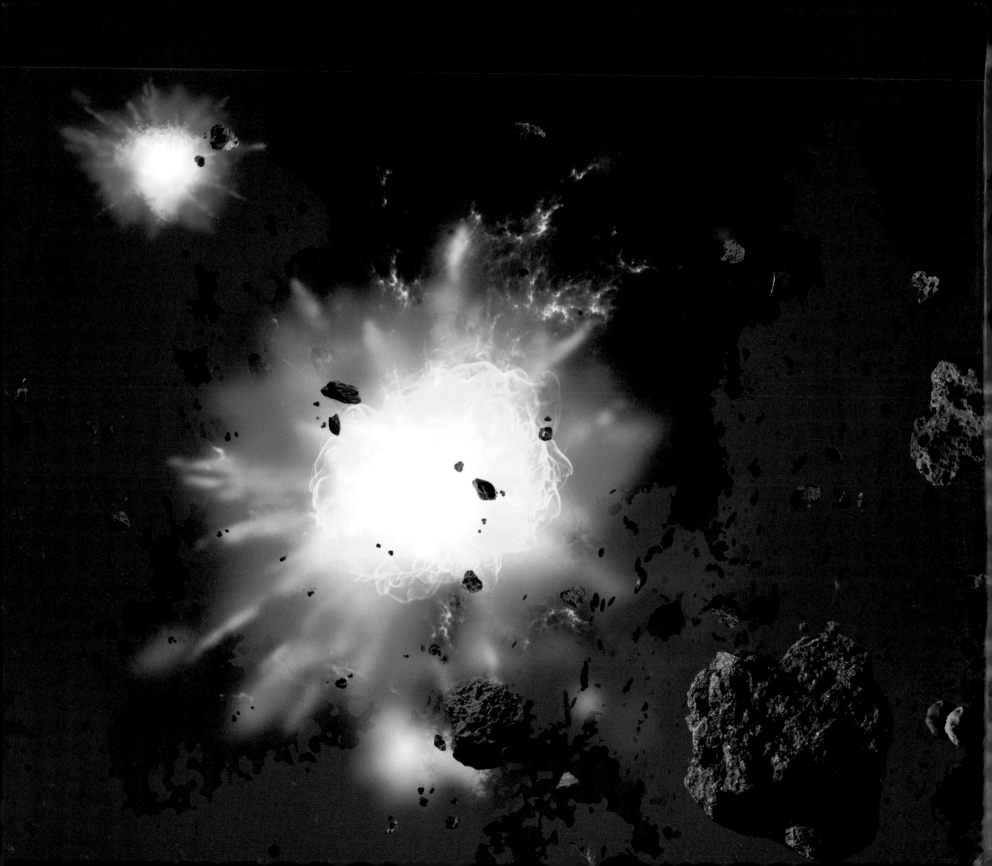

COSMIC CATASTROPHES

Seven Ways to Destroy a Planet Like Earth

DAVID A. AGUILAR

VIKING

This book is dedicated to my editor Sheila Keenan for her perseverance, laughter, and brilliant support; to Jim Hoover for his beautiful layout and inspired artistic art direction; and to my better half—Astrid (aka The Amazing Ms. Shirley, Queen of the Asteroids). It is also dedicated to all the young readers out there who sometimes stop and wonder "What if . . ."   — D.A.

VIKING
An imprint of Penguin Random House LLC
375 Hudson Street
New York, New York 10014

First published in the United States of America by Viking,
an imprint of Penguin Random House LLC, 2016

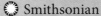 Smithsonian

SMITHSONIAN is a trademark owned by the Smithsonian Institution and is registered in the U.S. Patent and Trademark Office.

Smithsonian Enterprises:
Christopher Liedel, President
Carol LeBlanc, Senior Vice President, Education and Consumer Products
Brigid Ferraro, Vice President, Education and Consumer Products
Ellen Nanney, Licensing Manager
Kealy Gordon, Product Development Manager

Smithsonian National Air and Space Museum:
Andrew K. Johnston, Geographer, Center for Earth and Planetary Studies

LIBRARY OF CONGRESS CATALOGING-IN-PUBLICATION DATA
Names: Aguilar, David A., author.
Title: Cosmic catastrophes : seven ways to destroy a planet like earth / David Aguilar.
Description: New York : Viking, published by the Penguin Group, [2016] |
Audience: Ages 8-12. | Audience: Grades 4 to 6.
Identifiers: LCCN 2015044536 | ISBN 9780451476845 (hardcover)
Subjects: LCSH: Natural disasters—Juvenile literature. | Catastrophes (Geology)—Juvenile literature. | Planets—Juvenile literature. | Astronomy—Juvenile literature. | Earth (Planet)—Juvenile literature.
Classification: LCC GB5019 .A38 2016 | DDC 520—dc23 LC record available at http://lccn.loc.gov/2015044536

Manufactured in China   Set in Legacy and Classic Robot

10   9   8   7   6   5   4   3   2   1

Contents

Introduction

FOR THOSE READERS who like things that smash and crash and smoke and burn, this book is for you! For those readers who drive their parents and teachers crazy every time they start a sentence with the words, "What if . . ." this book is for you, too! And lastly, for those of you who have wondered why you cannot visit your local animal shelter and adopt a baby velociraptor, this book is really for you!

Why?

Because in the vast realm of outer space, accidents happen all the time. Things bump into other things. Stars blow up. Black holes snack on anything that crosses their paths. Space rocks the size of soccer fields smash into planets. Many of these events could change or eliminate all life on a world like Earth.

Can't happen to us, you say? Then you are going to be surprised to discover some of these accidents have already taken place. What follows is a very realistic and scientifically accurate description of what the future might hold for our favorite planet.

So please put your Crime Scene Investigation white laboratory coat on, roll up your sleeves, and get ready to investigate the most intriguing cosmic catastrophes that could ever happen to a planet. (If you do not own a starched white laboratory coat, a clean white T-shirt will work just as well!)

Earth-like planets found in the Milky Way galaxy appear in a variety of sizes and compositions.

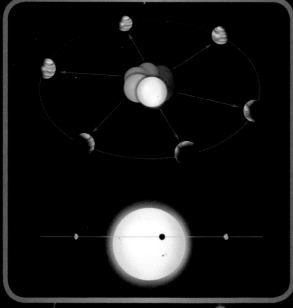

Astronomers can detect different-sized planets orbiting distant stars by seeing the stars wobble as the orbiting planets pull on them or by watching the light from a distant star dim as the planet passes in front of it.

WE ARE HERE

Welcome to our universe. From countless stars, galaxies, beautiful clouds of gas and dust, right down to the smallest subatomic particles and mysterious dark matter, the universe is the total of everything that exists. If it celebrated birthdays, it would be 13.8 billion years old. That's a lot of candles to put on a birthday cake! The universe was born right after the event astronomers call the Big Bang. Prior to that, nobody knows if anything existed. That's really hard to imagine, isn't it?

Our solar system, including the sun, formed about 4.5 billion years ago. Simple forms of life on Earth have existed for at least 3.6 billion years. If we do the math: universe (13.8 billion) minus solar system (4.5 billion), we realize Earth and the rest of our solar system missed out on more than 9 billion years of activity. A lot of stars and planets came and went during this time before we joined the party!

Recently, we have come to understand that the universe is very prolific, spinning out large numbers of planets, including ones like our own Earth. In our Milky Way galaxy alone, there may be more than 20 billion Earth-like worlds orbiting distant stars, and our Milky Way galaxy is just one of more than 225 billion other galaxies we can see in space.

Not only is the universe big, it is a marvelously chaotic place full of collisions, explosions, and searing blasts of radiation from dying stars. New stars and planets are born as older ones cease to be and slip into darkness. Wherever astronomers look with their telescopes, chaos reigns. Life, death, and change are ongoing events in our universe. What happens to planets like Earth is subject to chance and numerous possible outcomes. Some are favorable to life, others not so much. Big changes may occur over extremely long periods of time; others, like this supernova explosion, can happen quite abruptly.

The Earth is unlike any other planet in our solar system. It is a world rich with interdependent life in every imaginable place. Single-celled organisms can be found living inside rocks buried 12 miles (19 km) underground. Bizarre forms of life inhabit our seas and oceans, lakes and rivers. Earth's rocky continents are vibrant with life, and so is its atmosphere. Five miles above the surface of Earth, bacteria have been collected living in the clouds.

Life appeared on Earth after it cooled down enough for oceans to form. Life began with simple forms that became more complex over time. We know major planetary events can change or destroy life on a planet, but did you know life could change planets, too?

When single-celled life first appeared in our oceans, our planet would have been a very hostile, poisonous environment for us. We would not have been able to survive in the methane-gas-filled atmosphere. But over time, green plants multiplied in large numbers, removing carbon dioxide and methane gases from the atmosphere and replacing them with oxygen. Good for us in the long run; not so good for the first life-forms on Earth. Oxygen turned out to be poison to them, and soon oxygen-breathing organisms replaced them. In this instance, life altered a planet. Lucky for us! We wouldn't be here if this change had not occurred.

The atmosphere of ancient Earth did not contain much oxygen. Two billion years ago, green plants (below) using sunlight for photosynthesis appeared. They generated oxygen, which was destructive to the early red bacteria life (left).

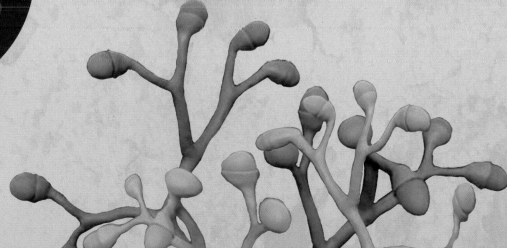

LEFT: The first simple life-forms on Earth colored the oceans red.

Look around you. It's very hard to imagine our world looking much different than it does today. Yet if you had a time machine and could travel millions of years into the past or the future, the geological and biological landscape would appear almost alien to our eyes. Humans or most of the plants and animals we see around us today might not be part of it.

Life on a planet may be diverse and widespread, but it can also be quite fragile. There have been five major mass extinction events on Earth where large numbers of species have disappeared. The most extreme of these was the Permian extinction 252 million years ago that wiped out 96 percent of life on Earth; only 4 percent of all living things remained behind to start over.

Slowly changing environmental conditions such as ice ages, massive volcanic eruptions, or explosive events like asteroid hits can all devastate a world like ours. What might some of these startling dramatic events look like if they happened today?

Get ready to investigate seven intriguing Cosmic Catastrophes! Coming soon—though probably not *too* soon—to an Earth-like planet near you!

Asteroid Hit

FEBRUARY 13, 2014, DAWN. The people of Chelyabinsk Oblast in the southern Ural region of Russia were just starting their morning—drinking coffee, driving to work, getting ready for a new school day. Suddenly a brilliant fireball streaked across the sky. It shone thirty times brighter than the sun and left a long trail of smoke and dust behind it . . . and then there was a deafening blast!

A shockwave smashed into the ground, injuring close to 1,500 people and damaging some 7,200 buildings. Panic broke out; what had been a peaceful town moments earlier now resembled a war zone. Roofs of buildings collapsed, windows were shattered, shards of glass and rubble lay everywhere. People later said the air smelled like "gunpowder" or "burning odors."

The fireball that hit Chelyabinsk Oblast was a chunk of rock about 65 feet (20 m) in diameter that exploded before it reached the ground. Traveling close to 40,000 miles per hour (64,000 km/hr), it released the explosive equivalent of 500,000 tons of TNT—almost thirty times as much energy as that generated by the atomic bomb dropped on Hiroshima during World War II.

The idea that rocks from outer space can pelt Earth is nothing new. Every day anywhere from 5 to 300 tons of space rocks and metal fragments hit our atmosphere, leaving white streaking trails behind them. The result is that Earth continuously gets heavier, gaining about 40,000 tons, or the equivalent of the weight of two aircraft carriers, every year. Want to see some of this debris coming in? Next time you are away from city lights at night, lie back on the ground and look up at the sky. As your eyes get adjusted to the darkness, you may suddenly see a streak or flash of light. There it is: a space rock hitting the Earth's upper atmosphere and flaming across the night sky as a meteor.

As spectacular as meteors might be, these are not the objects we need to worry about. The space rocks that do real damage, called asteroids, are the leftover building materials from when our early solar system formed 4.5 billion years ago. Most asteroids are found in an area between Mars and Jupiter called the asteroid belt. However, thousands of rogue asteroids called Near Earth Objects (NEOs) zip past Earth all the time. Some even pass between Earth and the moon. The realization that large asteroids may have affected life on Earth is relatively new.

Sixty-five million years ago (this sounds like a really long time ago, but in the history of the Earth it is not) the longest-living group of animals ever to walk the Earth disappeared. Suddenly there were no more bellowing dinosaurs, no more soaring pterodactyls, no more giant dragonflies or delicate sea creatures that we study as fossils today; the Earth was wiped clean of 70 percent of all life. Scientists had many theories as to why this happened, but they had no proof.

In 1980, that changed.

Paleontologists searching for fossils north of Rome, Italy, discovered something quite remarkable. Digging along a rocky hillside, they realized all the dinosaur fossils stopped when they reached a 1 inch (25 mm) thick layer of gray-colored clay sediment. Above this layer, all they found were fossils of mammals. This mysterious deposit seemed to mark the end of the dinosaurs and the beginning of a different kind of dominant life on our planet. Samples brought into the laboratory revealed the layer was mostly made of an element called iridium. Where did it come from, and why was this same layer found all over the Earth? Suddenly, it all became clear to scientists.

Iridium is extremely rare on Earth—but many asteroids contain large amounts of it. This layer found in Italy came from a mountain-sized asteroid striking Earth 66 million years ago. But where did

Near Earth Objects are asteroids that may pose a threat to life on Earth.

This layer of iridium clay was deposited on
Earth by an asteroid 66 million years ago.

this asteroid hit? Geologists searching for oil off the coast of the Yucatan Peninsula in Mexico had the answer. Two years earlier, they had discovered an underwater crater, 110 miles (180 km) in diameter and 12 miles (20 km) deep that was about 66 million years old. Twelve times deeper than the Grand Canyon, it was the largest confirmed impact crater on Earth. This is where the asteroid hit that ended the age of the dinosaurs, by throwing dust into the atmosphere, blocking sunlight and changing the global climate. Today we call it the K-T Event, named for the Cretaceous Tertiary period that marks the disappearance of the dinosaurs and the emergence of large mammals. (Scientists labeled the Cretaceous period "K" because of its spelling in German.) Now you're probably wondering: What are the chances an asteroid this size or bigger could hit Earth again? And, if it did, what would happen to us? Using what we know about the dinosaurs, let's investigate.

The asteroid that sent the dinosaurs on their way measured 3 to 10 miles (5 to 15 km) in diameter. This may seem large, but in comparison to other asteroids in the asteroid belt, it's not.

When an asteroid collision occurs, it's not the explosion that creates all the damage. It's the fires, dust, and burning debris raining down after the initial blast.

Imagine the scene: maybe it's early morning in the prehistoric neighborhood. On the banks of a shallow lake, a small herd of apatosauruses majestically dip their heads underwater, pulling up tasty plant morsels from the muddy bottom. On the shoreline, a stegosaurus mother watches over her newborn baby, while pterodactyls circle lazily overhead.

Suddenly the sky flashes blindingly white; flames and billowing black smoke follow, engulfing the horizon and racing outward in every direction. Within seconds the sky turns an eerie glowing red. A shockwave traveling more than 300 miles per hour (480 km/hr) levels the landscape. Falling trees burst into flame; rocks and soil ejected by the blast fall back down to the ground, burying the landscape under tons of mud. Fireballs rain down from the sky, igniting firestorms that blaze across the planet. Anything living caught above ground is incinerated. Tidal waves 150 feet (46 m) high flood the landscape, sweeping rocks, boulders, and trees along with them. Smoke and dust choke the skies, turning them pitch black.

Bright sunlight does not reach the ground again for months. Plants using photosynthesis, which requires sunlight, die. Acid rain falls silently to the ground, killing any remaining plants still struggling to survive. Freezing temperatures are the norm for the next three years. Life on Earth is changed forever. Gone are the majestic dinosaurs, monsters of the seas, and featherless flying reptiles. What remains is a slowly recovering world that soon will have different life on it.

Gigantic tidal waves appeared after the asteroid impact.

what are the chances this could happen to us? Luckily, they are slim. On average, big asteroids like the one that wiped out the dinosaurs 65 million years ago hit every 100 million years. That's not to say that something could not suddenly surprise us. A critical role some astronomers play today is the detection of asteroids long before they get here, so that something might be done to prevent a collision. For example, if we had a few years to respond, we might send a robotic spacecraft to gently nudge the asteroid onto another course so it would miss Earth completely.

For the past sixteen years, NASA has been monitoring the skies looking for asteroids larger than a half mile (almost 1 km) in diameter that might threaten our planet. So far they have found ninety of these big objects, but many more may be lurking out there undetected. Recently, researchers have been studying Asteroid 1950 DA. It appears that this large asteroid might be on a collision course with Earth, and it potentially has the capability of wiping us out if it hits on March 16, 2880. The chances right now are one in three hundred that it will hit us. Of course, by about 864 years from now, we should have technologies in place to protect our planet. However, the Earth has been hit many times in the past, and it will get hit again in the future. So if a rogue asteroid approaching Earth from the direction of the sun catches us by surprise . . . watch out!

Comet Swarm Collision

DATELINE: MARCH 24, 1993, San Diego County, California: Huddled around the glow of their computer screens in the Palomar Observatory, three astronomers sensed something was very wrong. They had been tracking a comet that had become trapped in orbit around Jupiter.

Then the comet disappeared—and what appeared was a total surprise, something that had never been seen before.

In its place were twenty-one smaller comets with long icy tails extending behind them. The astronomers realized the original comet had fragmented into pieces and soon would collide with our largest planet!

This was the first observation humans ever made of a cosmic collision within our solar system. Giant telescopes on Earth and in space were trained on Jupiter as the event unfolded. Traveling at more than 134,000 miles per hour (216,000 km/hr) the fragments plunged, one by one, into the upper atmosphere of this frozen gas giant. Dark scars larger than our moon appeared across the face of Jupiter and remained there for months. The amount of energy released by this collision was equal to 6 million tons of explosive TNT, or 600 times more powerful than all the nuclear weapons ever built. Can you imagine what might have happened if these fragments had—dare we think it—hit Earth?

Comets have been called "dirty snowballs," but they are really gigantic celestial icebergs. Most of them originate in the farthest region of our solar system in an area called the Oort Cloud, which is part of the original nebula or swirling cloud of gas and dust that gave birth to our solar system. Oort Cloud comets complete orbits around the sun measured in thousands of years, so once they appear we don't see them again in our lifetimes. The great comet Hale-Bopp was a spectacular sight seen around the world in 1997. Hale-Bopp came from the Oort Cloud, and it won't be seen again until the year 4385.

Closer in to our sun, another major group of comets originate from the Kuiper Belt, an area that stretches from the orbit of Pluto out beyond toward the Oort Cloud. The comets in this group are called short-period comets because they complete an orbit around the sun in less than 200 years. The famous Halley's Comet is a short-period comet that returns to our skies once every 75 or 76 years. Last seen in 1986, its next expected visit is in 2062.

Composed of loose sand, rock, water ice, and carbon dioxide, comets begin to defrost as they zip past the orbit of Jupiter, traveling in toward the sun. Then hurling across the orbit of Mars, they begin exhibiting a central glowing halo and contrails of gas and dust. Blown along by solar space winds, most comet tails move like wind vanes and point away from the sun.

Throughout history, comets have been described as flaming daggers or swords sent to warn us of some imminent danger or disaster. When Halley's Comet appeared in 1066, many believed it foretold the defeat of the mighty Saxon King Harold in the historic Battle of Hastings in England. (King Harold did lose the battle, but it wasn't because of the comet.)

When Halley's Comet appeared in 1910, astronomers discovered cyanogen gas, a poison, in the comet's tail. Many people panicked; they thought the vapors would suffocate everyone on Earth. They stuffed rags under the doors and in cracks around windows in their houses to keep the toxic vapors out. Churches were packed to the rafters with people who feared the impending visit from this comet signaled the end of the world. Astronomers tried to soothe the public, telling them there was nothing to fear. The nucleus, or solid head of the comet, would pass safely by, 24 million miles beyond Earth, and the tail was harmless. (However, if the nucleus of Halley's Comet had collided with the Earth, this story would have had a very different ending—*ka-pow!*)

Comets are mostly ice, dust, and rocks, with long tails stretching millions of miles through space.

An approaching doomsday comet would bring showers of meteors just before it hit Earth or other planets.

The Earth has been the bull's-eye target for comets many times in the past. Evidence has been found for more than 180 impacts on Earth's surface. These may have mostly been meteorites, but there have undoubtedly been comet impacts as well. Recent discoveries have suggested that a comet collided with our planet 13,000 years ago over central Mexico, where researchers uncovered the remains of melted rocks and microscopic diamonds that could only have formed under the extreme pressures of the ancient atmospheric explosion of a comet.

Earth's most recent dust-up with a comet may have occurred in a remote area of Siberia called Tunguska. On June 30, 1908, a little after seven in the morning, Russian settlers near Lake Baikal were startled to see a bluish light brighter than the sun pass across the sky. Ten minutes later they heard and felt the blast! A witness, blown out of his chair while sitting on the front porch of a store, said the sky split in half and the entire top of the sky appeared to be on fire; a crash of stones falling from the sky rapidly followed. The Earth shook and trembled violently. The unseated Russian said it was so hot it felt like his shirt was on fire. The explosion from this event leveled 80 million trees over 1,830 square miles (4,740 sq km), an area larger than the state of Rhode Island! Trees at the epicenter of the blast resembled bare telephone poles. Absolutely all bark and branches were stripped away. They looked eerily like the trees later seen at 1950s atmospheric nuclear test sites.

Was it a comet or a meteoroid that detonated in the air above Siberia in 1908? This is still a topic of great debate among researchers; however, the extent of damages mirrors what we would expect a comet fragment to leave behind in a collision with Earth.

RIGHT: This photograph of Tunguska was taken by Russian scientists nineteen years after a probable comet impact in 1908.

We would certainly know of a possible comet event in advance. In the twenty-first century, scientists around the world track and monitor asteroids, comets, and NEOs every day. In the event of a predicted collision with a comet, we would have months or years to prepare. Most likely massive living shelters would be constructed underground or in hillsides to protect us from the fate that was rapidly approaching. Visible in the daytime sky, the comet would grow increasingly larger and brighter. As the day of impact drew near, our skies would begin radiating meteor storms, flashing in every direction as small debris pushed ahead of the comet's icy nucleus hit our upper atmosphere. Ultimately, a sudden blinding flash would fill the sky, followed by a thundering roar. The sky would turn into a sheet of fire! A heat wave 12,000°F (6,650°C) would sweep across the surface of the planet incinerating everything in its path. The surfaces of oceans would boil. An electromagnetic pulse released by the explosion would destroy all electrical devices. No more cell phones, TVs, cars, subways, streetlights, elevators, or gas stations pumping fuel—nothing that runs on electricity would work. The only bright lights visible would be the colorful red and green aurora dancing across the night skies. Earth would grow dark and silent without electricity. People emerging from the deep underground shelters would shiver in the cold arctic temperatures due to clouds of dust and debris blocking the sunlight. They would not recognize the scorched landscape where no animals roamed, no birds sang songs, no flowers bloomed. Survival would be difficult.

How likely is an event of this magnitude? Scary, but decidedly rare. Comets have hit our planet in the past, and projections show more will do so in the future. The probability of a major collision is actually quite small for the next several hundred years. But we don't know for sure, so keep watching the skies!

Thrown Out of the Solar System

IMAGINE YOURSELF as a planet that gets kicked out of your solar system. Orbital weirdness! In the past ten years astronomers have discovered planets can actually change their orbits over time. Take the case of dwarf planet Pluto. Today we find it traveling in a very odd elliptical orbit around the sun. But that wasn't always Pluto's path. The gravitational influences of Neptune appear to have pushed the dwarf planet into a new location.

In solar systems around distant stars, it is common to find gas giant planets where they should not be. After forming in the cold remote region of their solar system, at some point these solitary wanderers moved closer to their star where it was warmer. Many of these planets went a little too far in. We call them "Hot Jupiters" because their orbits are so close to their suns that they become fiery gas balls zooming around their stars. For example, Mercury orbits the sun every 88 days. Hot Jupiters can orbit their stars in under 20 hours! That's a precariously fast year. So could planets jostling about our own solar system pose a threat to Earth? Let's explore how this might occur.

We perceive the planets circling our sun in round paths that never change shape or position. On this point, we would be incorrect. Planets can experience orbital changes for many different reasons. Early on in the chaotic formation of solar systems, planets can be banged around a lot. As our own solar system came together, Earth collided with a wandering Mars-sized object. Debris that was hurled into space formed a beautiful ring around our planet. Can you imagine seeing Earth with a halo ring? Fortunately for us, that halo was short-lived. The particles tumbled together and grew in size, forming our moon; this stabilized the rotation of our planet, helping life to begin.

So now we ask: What would cause a gas giant planet to creep into our cosmic neighborhood? A passing star or mini black hole could do it. When you are viewing the nighttime summer sky, there is an old saying that helps identify a very bright and peculiar star. Locate the Big Dipper. Then starting at the four stars in the dipper bowl, move your extended finger along the handle in a gentle arc until you "arc on to Arcturus," a brightly colored orange star. Incredibly, Arcturus is cutting through the Milky Way. Either it is a member of a small group of stars that may have been part of another galaxy that long ago collided and merged with the Milky Way, or it may have been dislodged from the outer regions of our galaxy. This means that any planets that might have been orbiting Arcturus may now be drifting all alone through space.

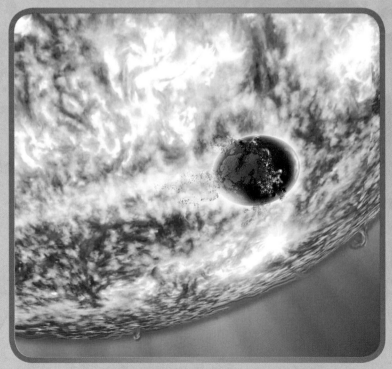

A planet falling into its star is stretched and pulled apart by gravity, with a cometary tail trailing behind.

RIGHT: If a gas giant planet moves past a smaller planet, it could be bombarded by the gas giant's smaller moons.

There are between 200 to 400 billion stars in our Milky Way galaxy. If a wandering star were to pass too close to our solar system, its gravitational field might nudge one of the outer gas giant planets in toward our sun. As the gas giant powered its way through the inner solar system, the orbits of the smaller inner rocky worlds could become chaotic. Mars, Earth, Venus, and Mercury could be forced into the sun's blazing inferno. It may sound extraordinary, but the Earth could be reunited with the star that gave it birth. Alternatively, we could end up being thrown completely out of our solar system! Without a sun to heat our world, surface life on Earth would perish very quickly.

In the future, other fates may also be in store for our planet. Galaxies are massive cities of stars that come in a variety of shapes. Our Milky Way galaxy has a beautiful spiral shape. One of our closest galactic neighbors is the Andromeda galaxy, another spiral galaxy containing close to a trillion stars. Four billion years from now (remember this date and write it down somewhere so you won't be surprised), astronomers calculate these two galaxies are destined to collide. This is very common with galaxies. We see collisions going on everywhere we look in space. When our galaxy collides with Andromeda, there is a chance that Earth will be kicked out into space. If we are fortunate, our sun will travel right along with us and we will survive this collision. Life won't be altered dramatically. The all-new "Milkomeda" galaxy (Milky Way and Andromeda galaxies combined) will become a much brighter river of stars across our night sky. But if our planet is stripped away from the sun, life on our world will have a much different destiny.

Stretched, cracked, and broken by the extreme gravitational field
of our sun, Earth might be pulled inside it and disappear forever.

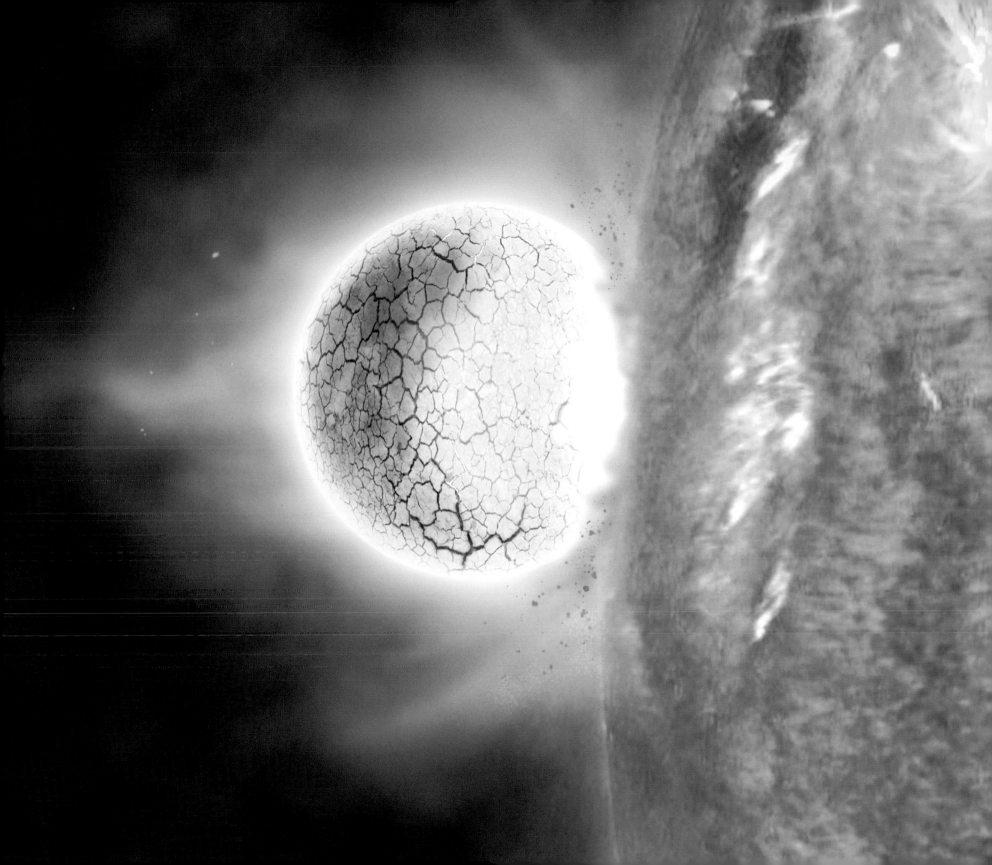

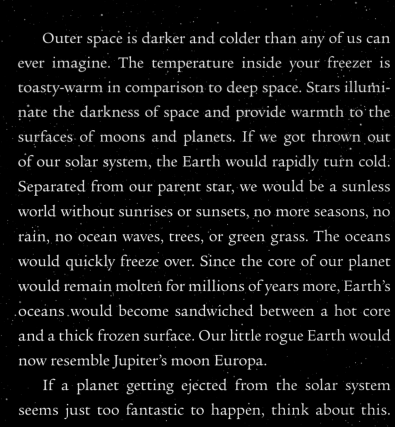

Outer space is darker and colder than any of us can ever imagine. The temperature inside your freezer is toasty-warm in comparison to deep space. Stars illuminate the darkness of space and provide warmth to the surfaces of moons and planets. If we got thrown out of our solar system, the Earth would rapidly turn cold. Separated from our parent star, we would be a sunless world without sunrises or sunsets, no more seasons, no rain, no ocean waves, trees, or green grass. The oceans would quickly freeze over. Since the core of our planet would remain molten for millions of years more, Earth's oceans would become sandwiched between a hot core and a thick frozen surface. Our little rogue Earth would now resemble Jupiter's moon Europa.

If a planet getting ejected from the solar system seems just too fantastic to happen, think about this. Astronomers have already identified a distant orphan planet skipping along among the stars, and there may be billions more of these lonely travelers out there. Could this happen to Earth? For now our place in the universe is secure. No stars have been detected that could start this type of chain reaction . . . and at least we have several billion years until the collision of the Milky Way and Andromeda galaxies may occur.

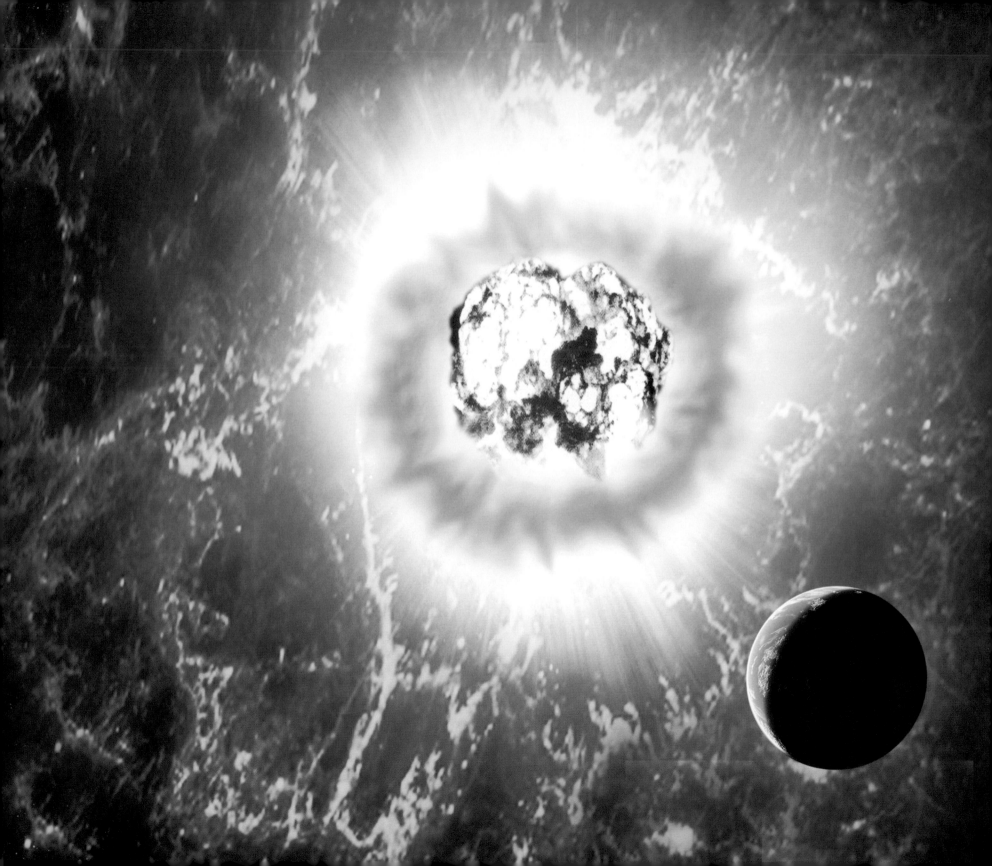

Supernova Explosion

WHEN WE GAZE at the Milky Way and twinkling stars at night, nothing appears to change. The same stars and constellations remain year after year. Occasionally an exceptionally bright meteor may streak across the sky, or the moon may morph into a coppery-red hue during a lunar eclipse, but our stars and planets reign on, and nothing too much seems out of place or new. But as astronomers and amateur sky watchers know, changes are ongoing. Some happen over millions or even billions of years and others occur in just one night. There is no better example of this than the sudden appearance of a magical, mystical supernova.

In 1572, the Danish astronomer Tycho Brahe gazed skyward night after night, focused on a dazzling star that had materialized in the night sky. Where nothing had been seen before, there now blazed a sparkling newcomer with light more intense than the planet Venus. It was called a *nova stella* or "new star" in Latin. Brahe was not alone in marveling at this new celestial guest. From China to the plains of the American southwest, night sky observers wondered with awe at this new apparition. Incredibly, nearly four centuries passed before anyone knew that this luminous star was actually a supernova. When a star burns through its supply of nuclear fuel as it reaches the end of its life cycle, it can suddenly send a blast across the universe, releasing spectacular energy. Sounds exciting, doesn't it?

A supernova explosion results when a giant star suddenly collapses under gravity's commanding pressure and blasts itself into space. For a brief period of time the supernova may outshine every other star in the sky. After this violent event, within days or weeks these stellar remains slowly fade away, virtually disappearing from view. Left behind is a ragged cloud of expanding gas and dust known as a supernova remnant. Today, we see many supernova remnants spread out across space. Even though no stars going supernova have been observed in the Milky Way since the invention of the telescope in 1609, this does not mean one could not explode tomorrow. In the process of destroying themselves and everything around them, supernovas also create new stars and planets from the debris thrown out into space. In doing so they bring about life and death all at once. Should a supernova detonate anywhere near us, it could spell trouble for life here on Earth.

Exploding supernovas can send out deadly gamma rays that sweep across space destroying any life they encounter on a planet.

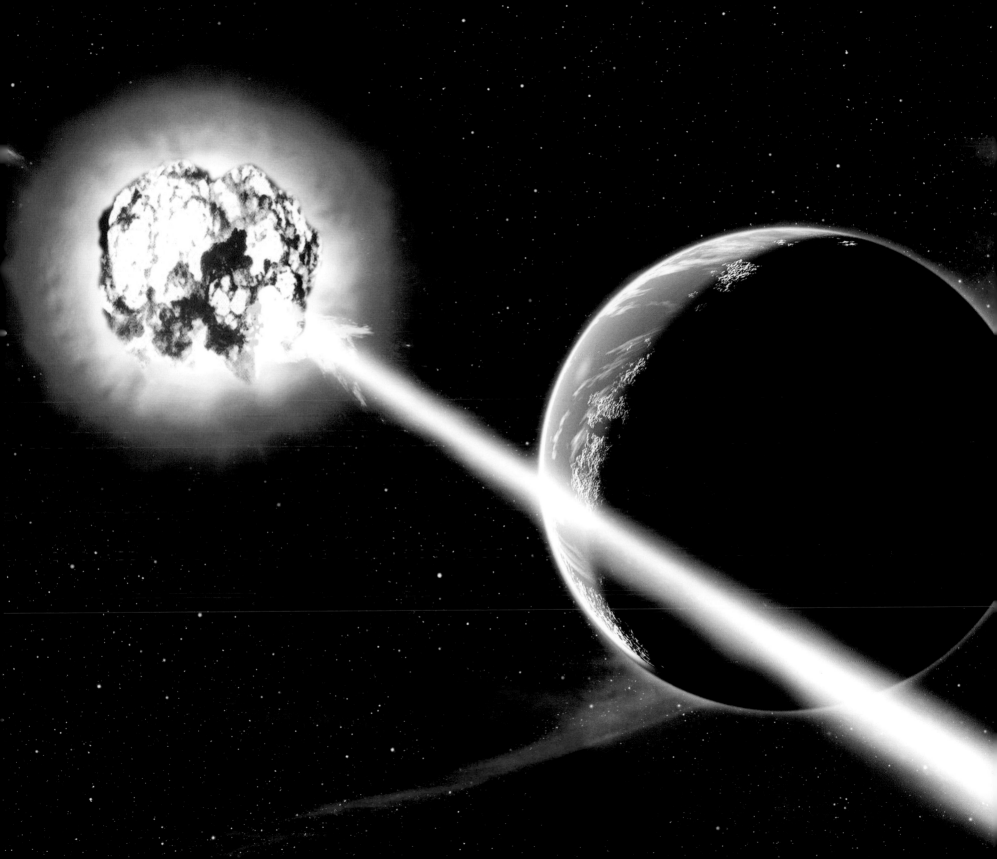

Are there any star candidates in our night sky primed to become a supernova? Interestingly, the answer is yes, and some of these potential "space bombs" are well known to astronomers. Let's begin with a wintertime favorite. In the constellation Orion the Hunter, the star forming his left shoulder is a very bright red gem named Betelgeuse, pronounced "Beetle-juice."

Betelgeuse is a red giant star located 600 light years away from Earth, and it is running low on the hydrogen and helium gases that keep it burning. It is inevitable: someday Betelgeuse will collapse under its own weight and then rebound to light up our night sky in a spectacular explosion, becoming the brightest visible object besides the sun and moon.

However, astronomers are not as concerned about Betelgeuse as they are about the brilliant southern hemisphere double star Eta Carinae. Located 7,500 light years away from Earth, it is the next-best candidate to go supernova. Eta Carinae is so big that when one of these superstars blows, it will be visible in the daytime sky. Will Earth sustain damage from this event, or will we just be treated to the biggest fireworks show in the universe? Just as there's no way to predict when a pop quiz may happen at school, researchers say there is no way to tell when Eta Carinae will send a blast out across space and time.

The dying star Eta Carinae blasts out two billowing clouds of gas—a prelude to becoming a supernova.

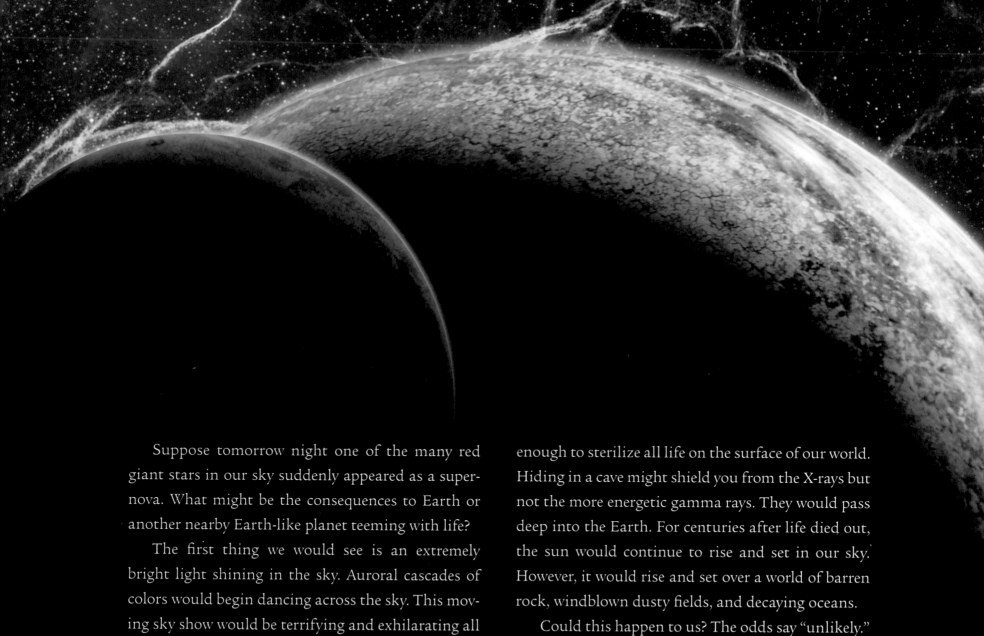

Suppose tomorrow night one of the many red giant stars in our sky suddenly appeared as a supernova. What might be the consequences to Earth or another nearby Earth-like planet teeming with life?

The first thing we would see is an extremely bright light shining in the sky. Auroral cascades of colors would begin dancing across the sky. This moving sky show would be terrifying and exhilarating all at the same time. Within hours, as this spectacular multicolored light show began fading, deadly X-rays and gamma rays would begin penetrating the atmosphere. This lethal combination might be strong enough to sterilize all life on the surface of our world. Hiding in a cave might shield you from the X-rays but not the more energetic gamma rays. They would pass deep into the Earth. For centuries after life died out, the sun would continue to rise and set in our sky. However, it would rise and set over a world of barren rock, windblown dusty fields, and decaying oceans.

Could this happen to us? The odds say "unlikely." We are more likely to be hit by an asteroid or comet. But on some other unlucky Earth-like planet out there, this could be happening right now as part of the everyday life in our universe.

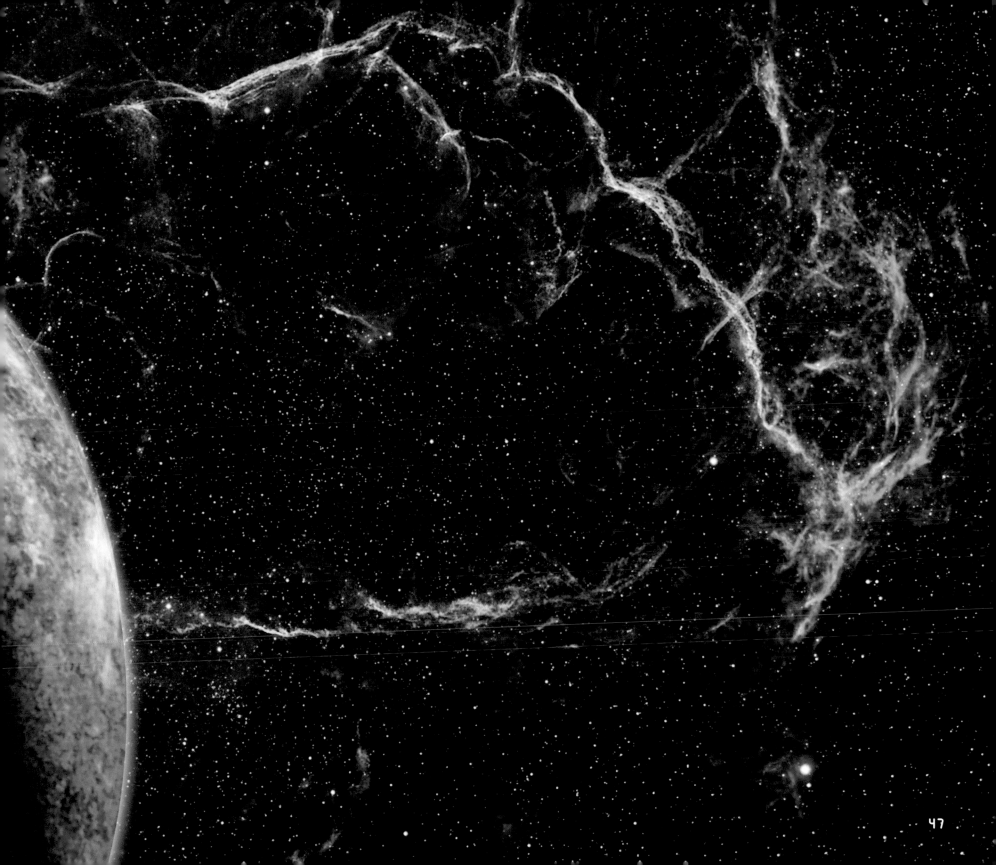

Swallowed by a Black Hole

BLACK HOLES ARE one of the most exotic objects in our universe. They form when the cores of massive stars collapse and disappear into oblivion. A black hole has the strongest gravitational field of any object in the universe. It's so strong and relentless, even light cannot escape it. A black hole is a dense, bottomless pit that goes nowhere, to a place we call a singularity. Although some stars orbit black holes and avoid being swallowed up, stars, planets, or solar systems unlucky enough to pass too close to a black hole's gravitational field get sucked in. Where do they end up? Unknown. But we do know one simple fact:

once something falls into a black hole, it never comes out, ever again.

Mathematics tells us that something odd happens to the passage of time in black holes. When a star or planet falls into a black hole, time apparently stops for that object: there is no yesterday, no tomorrow, only now. It seems to make no sense that a million years may pass back on Earth but not even a second has flown by inside the black hole. Weird? You bet. Black holes remain one of the universe's most bizarre objects ever discovered.

Black holes are the remains of the largest stars found in space. When very large stars run out of their nuclear fuel and begin collapsing, they do not explode. Instead they continue shrinking down until they disappear into something that is no longer visible. Astronomers locate them by identifying stars that emit energetic X-rays and appear distorted or stretched by something invisible. These space oddities come in three basic sizes. There are mini-sized black holes, medium-sized stellar black holes with 20 times more mass than our sun, and super-massive black holes that are found in the centers of galaxies. The biggest black hole ever discovered has more mass than 17 billion of our suns put together. In size it is eleven times larger than the diameter of Neptune's orbit around the sun. Not to be left out, our Milky Way galaxy has a monster black hole hidden in its center. During a warm summer evening, look at the part of the constellation Sagittarius sometimes called the "teapot." Right there, you are looking directly into the heart of our galaxy and the resident black hole hidden behind clouds of gas and dust.

Of the three different sizes, it's the stellar black holes we need to closely track. Unlike the static super-massive holes in the centers of galaxies, stellar black holes can wander undetected through space. Many people confuse wormholes with these black holes. Wormholes are said to be bridges that connect different locations in the universe by "bending" space-time and creating shortcuts for long boring journeys. Predicted by Einstein's general theory of relativity, they are frequently used in science-fiction movies to quickly go from one place to another.

When commanding space missions, every good starship captain knows black holes are the remains of collapsed stars. Their gravity is so great you may get locked in an orbit around one or be pulled inward and ripped apart. Scientists have no proof wormholes exist, but they certainly know black holes are real.

It's a fact: there are a lot of black holes on the loose in space. NASA's Chandra X-ray Observatory has located thousands of them in the Milky Way alone, but

Black holes in the centers of galaxies emit powerful jets of material at nearly the speed of light.

there may be millions more that remain as yet undetected. Now, what would happen if one paid an unexpected visit to our solar system?

It might not be what you think.

Although a black hole would take a very long time to reach Earth, we would still be at a big disadvantage. The best optical telescopes, like the Hubble Space Telescope, would not be able to see it. But when an object like a star or planet falls into a black hole, kinetic X-rays are emitted. Scientists can detect X-rays emitted by a black hole in space, so if a black hole approached our solar system, they might pick it up. Too bad for us, there would be nothing we could do. It would be like waving your arms on a beach trying to stop a tidal wave. Good luck with that.

If a small stellar-sized black hole passed through the outer reaches of our solar system, far out in the fringes of the Oort Cloud, we might see swarms of new comets moving in toward the sun. We've already looked at the consequences of comets crashing into Earth. If the velocity of the black hole was high enough and it kept going along its journey through space, comets filling our skies might be the only thrill we would experience. If the Earth avoided any impacts, we would remain safe. The night sky would be mesmerizing with so many brilliant comets with long billowing tails spread across the starry landscape. This would be a sight no living creature on Earth had seen before or would likely ever see again.

As the black hole continued its wanderings, our solar system would settle back down to the way it had been before that unscheduled interruption. In this case, Earth would have dodged calamity and survived, with the greatest light show ever! Life would continue as usual—unless luck wasn't with us and the nomad black hole came barreling straight toward us.

First we'd be immersed in clouds of comets like swarms of angry bees stinging everything in sight. The strong gravitational field generated by the approaching black hole would disrupt the orbits of the outer planets, especially Neptune and Uranus, and the objects in the Kuiper Belt, like Pluto. We already know what can happen when the outer giant planets start shifting their orbits. Smaller rocky planets like our own Earth could get pushed into the sun or thrown out of the solar system. Closing in near the asteroid belt, our black hole would suddenly flare up and become visible to us as its gravity started bending light all around it. Saturn and Jupiter, although giants in our solar system, would be

If it was caught in the gravitational grip of a black hole, Earth would be pulled apart atom by atom before disappearing into it.

nothing compared to the mass of the encroaching black hole. Both planets would be ripped apart and disappear into the consuming cosmic monster.

With asteroids and comets now being hurtled toward us, our world could take devastating hits from space. Very quickly, Earth could turn into a glowing red sphere with volcanoes erupting and lava flowing over its entire surface. The same thing would happen to our moon and all the inner planets. What was left of our atmosphere would be pulled into the black hole, followed by our planet itself. Ripped to shreds right down to its atoms, the Earth would slide into the black hole never to be seen again.

Grim as all this might sound, this "visit" wouldn't be over yet. The sun, our star that held all the planets together, would be the next victim.

Pulled into the approaching black pit, what was left of the solar system would suddenly go dark. Finished with its meal, the black hole would become invisible again. Then, slightly larger after eating our solar system for lunch, it would continue its never-ending journey as it encountered other cosmic victims along the way. Life on Earth, or any other life-bearing world that was unlucky enough to meet a black hole, would now be history. There would be nothing left of Earth to show it existed except ancient radio broadcasts still traveling light years through space. Soon, they too would fade away. Other Earth-like planets may be getting torn apart as you read this right now. But fear not! Scientists do not see black holes as a threat to Earth, because the distances between us are just too great.

This rapidly approaching black hole would be a cosmic doomsday machine.

End of the Sun

ITS RADIANCE TAKES only eight minutes to travel 93 million miles (150 million km) across space to touch our cheeks and make us feel warm. We've grown accustomed to the presence of our nearest star, but we can still experience the awe of it at daybreak over the ocean, or watching it sink gently behind distant mountains framed in glorious clouds of orange, gold, red, and crimson. We miss it at night—the darkness can be filled with so many scary sounds made by things we cannot see without it. It is the anchor that holds our solar system together. Our sun is a star just like all the others that twinkle in our skies at night. However, the sun is essential: it provides the energy and light that supports life on our world.

Energy received from the sun powers most of the life found on Earth and possibly elsewhere in the solar system. Plants absorb energy from the sun, carbon dioxide gas from the atmosphere, and minerals dissolved in water from the soil. These are the essentials for them to grow and thrive. They then release oxygen gas back into the atmosphere as a waste product. Animals eat the plants, breathe in the oxygen, and exhale carbon dioxide back into the atmosphere. Life on Earth is a marvelous balanced cycle.

All stars in the universe including our sun have a lifetime clock that was set when they were formed. Like a lawnmower with only one tank of gas, when our

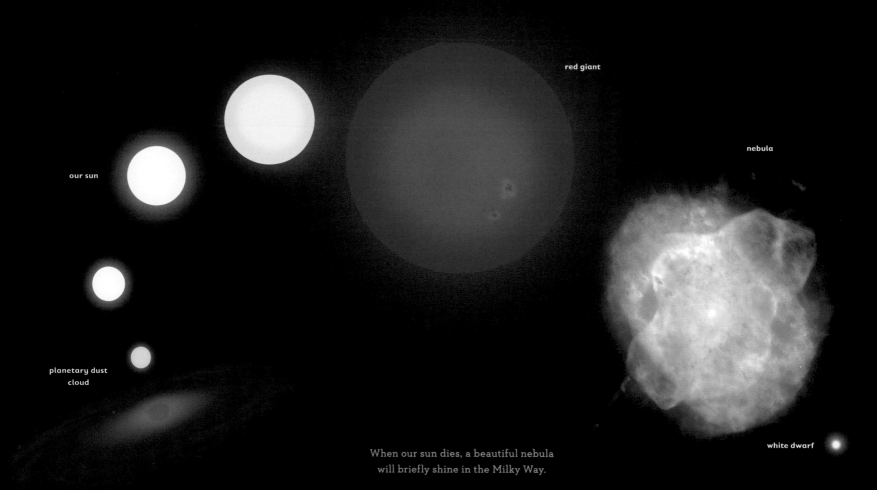

red giant

nebula

our sun

planetary dust
cloud

white dwarf

When our sun dies, a beautiful nebula
will briefly shine in the Milky Way.

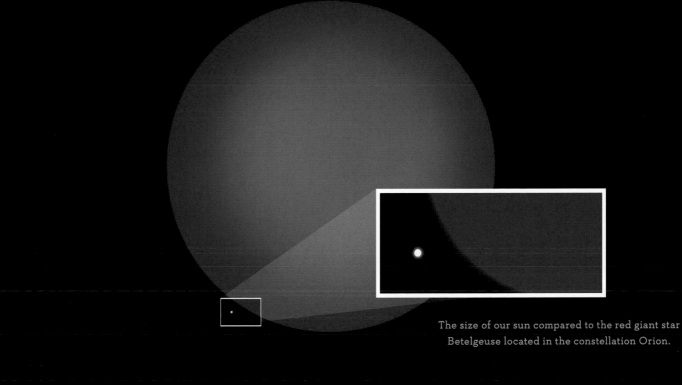

The size of our sun compared to the red giant star
Betelgeuse located in the constellation Orion.

sun runs out of fuel, it too will stop running. With this in mind, we know our sun will not be radiating heat and light forever. When our star passes into history, planet Earth will pass, too.

Our sun is about halfway through its life cycle and fuel supply. It and all the planets in our solar system were born out of a gigantic dust cloud 4.5 billion years ago. Astronomers know that deep inside our sun there is enough nuclear fuel to power it for another 4 to 5 billion years. That may seem like a very long time, but not when you're thinking in "universe time." (Remember: our universe is about 13.8 billion years old now.)

We learned earlier that big stars collapse when they run out of fuel, and then explode into supernovas. Monster stars do a vanishing act into black holes. Medium-size stars like our sun travel a calmer road in life. When these stars run out of nuclear fuel, they balloon out to become red giants. Over time, as they exhaust the rest of their fuel, they shrink back down, cramming all their leftover materials into a sphere the size of Earth. At this stage we call them "white dwarfs." They will remain white dwarf stars for millions of years before ultimately fading away. *Adios, amigos!*

Someday, our sun will become a red giant and may swell
in size to reach the orbit of the Earth and the moon.

Recently astronomers made a startling discovery. They calculated that 2.8 billion years from now our aging sun will grow so hot it will destroy all life on Earth. Even bacteria living miles underground will not survive. If we had a time machine to travel 2.8 billion years into the future, what would we see? We'd gaze upon a dead planet composed of rock, sand, and vast salt flats left behind by evaporated oceans.

As our sun ages and grows hotter and brighter, how will this affect life on our planet? First to go will be the land animals, as the Earth's surface becomes too hot for life to exist. Then all the sea creatures will disappear, as the oceans evaporate into space. (Every shark knows you can't swim if there isn't any water.) As the atmosphere grows hotter, more water vapor will form. Clouds will envelop our planet, dimming the light but not stopping the heat from entering. With more water vapor in the atmosphere, carbon dioxide will be lost to space. As the amount of available carbon dioxide dwindles, the few surviving plants will be the next to go. Without plants producing oxygen, it will become harder to breathe. Many futurists believe humans, who appeared relatively recently on Earth (a mere 3.5 million years ago), could also perish. Using various technologies, we may be able to hold off the inevitable for a while. With average daytime temperatures eventually reaching a scorching 167°F (75°C), it will be hot enough to bake a cake or slowly cook a turkey just by placing it outdoors in the sun. Initially, we may seek shelter underground during the day and venture out only at night when it is slightly cooler. Surveying the tortured landscape, we will see that Earth has become an uninhabitable planet. Migrating farther out to Mars or relocating to a new Earth-like world far beyond our solar system could be our only hope for survival. We may very well become starfarers in search of a new home.

As our dying sun swells, the Earth and moon
will become red, glowing spheres of rock.

Observed from a distance, the last days of our sun will be both beautiful and fascinating to watch as its life as a star comes to an end. There will be no violent explosions to shatter the backdrop of eternal space. A much different and gorgeous outcome awaits our star. As it struggles to continue shining during the red giant phase, its outer layers will separate and be blown away into space. It will form what astronomers call a planetary nebula. This odd name came from early astronomers stumbling upon distant round gas clouds that looked like ghostly planets. *Nebula* comes from the Greek word meaning "cloud." Planetary nebula have also been called cosmic tombstones marking the end of a star like our sun, or cosmic butterflies, because the nebula's wild shapes, bright colors, and short lifetimes remind us of a butterfly.

Visible for only a few thousand years, the shapes and colors of planetary nebula depend on how fast the original star was spinning before the red giant phase set in, or whether another passing star pulled on it in some way. When our sun passes on, billions of years from now, another intelligent civilization may glance skyward and record the discovery of a beautiful new planetary nebula in an arm of the Milky Way galaxy. This will be the last colorfully visible remains of our sun, slowly fading away into darkness. In its unique way, our cosmic butterfly bobbing alone across the Milky Way will confirm our star's existence. It will proclaim, for the next few thousand years, that we were here.

Planetary nebula come in a variety of shapes and colors.

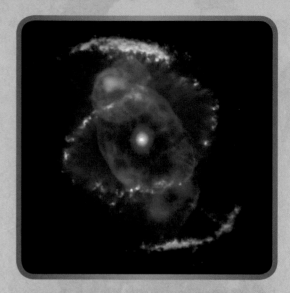

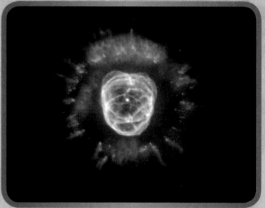

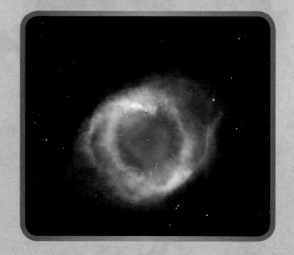

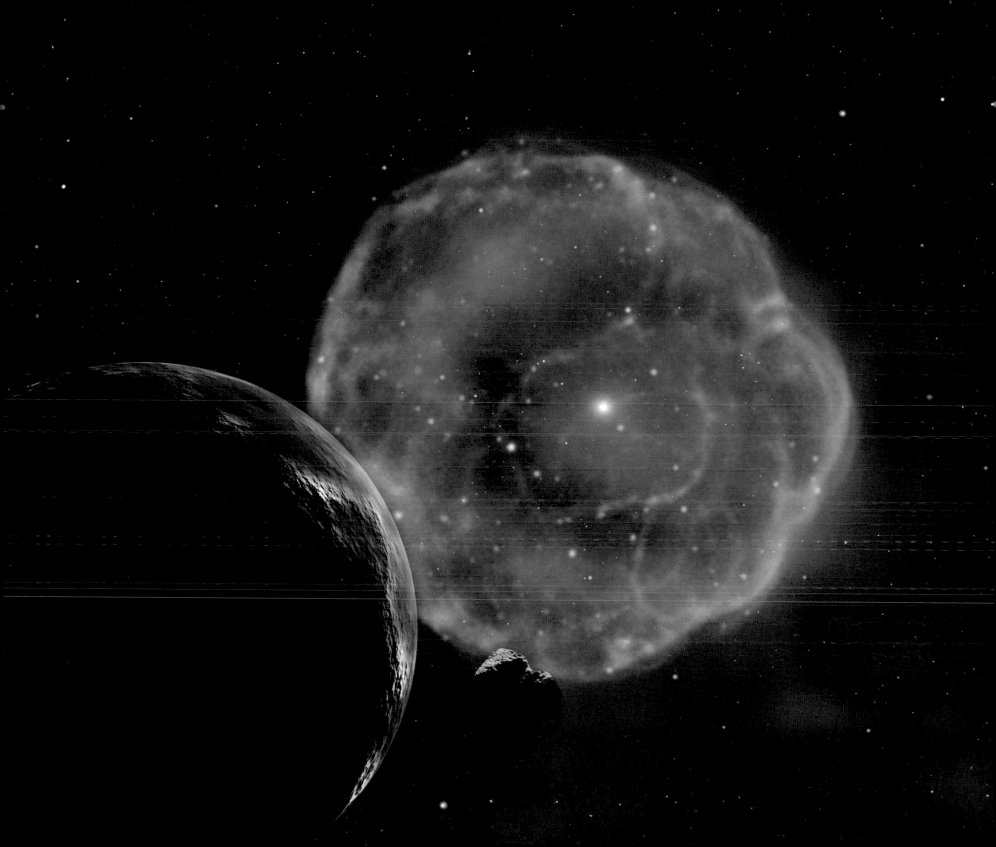

That Dreaded Alien Invasion!

IN MOVIES, COMIC BOOKS, video games, and on TV we frequently battle bad guys from outer space. Of all the cosmic catastrophes that might occur, escaping from alien invaders is the least likely to happen. So why is this theme of human vs. alien so popular? Our preoccupation with alien invasions may very well be based on human behavior throughout history, which includes a long line of wars, invasions, and colonization where various peoples conquered other peoples—often with superior weaponry—and then took their land, resources, or wealth, and sometimes enslaved the defeated group. Could modern people harbor the fear that somebody (or something) might treat us the same way—arriving in spaceships and using ray guns?

At the end of the nineteenth century, British author H. G. Wells wrote his classic book *The War of the Worlds*, describing an invasion of Earth by creatures from Mars. As a Halloween show in 1938, the actor and radio personality Orson Welles and his theater company read scripts based on this book and broadcast their drama as a "news bulletin" over the CBS radio station throughout the United States. Some radio listeners panicked! They didn't understand that they were hearing actors in a live radio play. What they heard was, "The Martians are coming!" Fearing for their lives, some people called the police and the newspapers, which then headlined the "panic" story. In rural communities more than one water tower was hit with buckshot fired by anxious hunters trying to stop imagined Martian walking machines headed for their town.

Were all those folks right to be worried? Well, not because of this radio broadcast. Many astronomers maintain that alien invasions are not a threat at all, due to the vast distances between the stars. Traveling at half the speed of light, it could take thousands of years to journey to Earth from another star. Unless aliens live for thousands of years, the distances involved do not appear to make long-distance spaceflight possible.

Another factor is the complexity and expense of an attempt to take over a planet. The energy and resources needed to travel between the stars would be much more costly than it would be to just alter a younger planet that's closer to the aliens' home. The strongest argument against alien visitors coming to battle Earth is called the Fermi Paradox. Our sun is a common type of star and a relative newcomer to the universe. There are millions of older stars like ours out there; some of them may have planets around them on which intelligent life may have evolved much earlier than it did on Earth. Some of that evolved life should be capable of space travel. Earth then should have been visited or attacked ages ago by starfaring aliens, but we see no signs of this. This prompted the famous Italian physicist Enrico Fermi to ask a very simple but powerful question: "Where is everybody?" This is the Fermi Paradox.

Dr. Stephen J. Hawking.

A very different view, however, comes from the well-known contemporary British physicist Stephen Hawking. He believes intelligent alien life almost certainly exists in space, and trying to communicate with it is too risky. In Hawking's own words, "We only have to look at ourselves to see how intelligent life might develop into something we wouldn't want to meet."

Might aliens be interested in our tiny blue planet? It could be a tempting target from which to collect natural resources such as water or metals needed by alien civilizations that have exhausted all of their own natural resources. If an alien planet experienced a cosmic catastrophe from a nearby supernova, or if their sun was turning into a red giant, they might look elsewhere for a new home. If any of these situations brought massive spaceships to our skies, there is something else to consider that stories and film rarely present. To begin with, there is no biological reason beings from space would look anything like us, with a head on top of their shoulders complemented by two eyes, two ears, a nose, and a mouth. When humans meet on a battlefield, they have some sense of recognition or connection with their human enemies. But how would we reason with something that might look like a giant fungus with green tentacles and communicate in ways we can't understand?

Alien life may be stranger than anything we can ever imagine.

Let's say scientists have overestimated the unimaginable distances of space travel and the resources needed to fly between the stars, and aliens of evil intent cast shadows down from our skies. To move humans off the planet, what tactics might they use? Instead of an outright military attack, more evolved beings might first generate a huge electromagnetic pulse directed at Earth's surface. This would overload and blow out all of the electrical circuits on our planet. Global communications would cease. All tweets would come to a standstill. Airplanes could not fly. Pumps would stop dispensing water or gasoline, food would cease being transported to markets, and all cities would go dark. The second phase of a coordinated attack might be the release of deadly short-lived viruses into our atmosphere that were genetically engineered to specifically infect and eliminate humans. Many animals might also suffer, but to certain pyramid-shaped creatures with six green tentacles and fourteen light sensory organs, so what? To the invading aliens this would be part of their plan to change the Earth and start over.

After these first waves of attack, the door-to-door clean-up ray gun battles might begin. A scenario like this would devastate much of the life on our planet. After the alien invaders had cleared the landscape, they would set up their own cities and begin a new life on a planet that used to be called Earth. However, here's the really interesting part. Although humans might be gone, bacteria and viruses living in our soils, rocks, and oceans would remain. This could be Earth's last best defense against alien invaders, and the consequences could eliminate them quite rapidly. It's not likely aliens from another planet would have immunities to Earth's minor maladies including flu, whooping cough, or even the common cold. Within a few months, the invaders could be wiped out, too. With the aliens defeated by the smallest living things on Earth, including germs, viruses, and bacteria, our world could be green again, flowers would bloom, and life would go on . . . peacefully awaiting the next would-be conquerors from space.

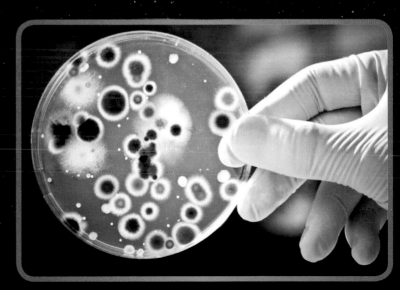

A technician holds a petri dish thriving with bacteria, the most common life-forms on Earth. Bacteria could potentially cause

"I am tormented with an everlasting itch for things remote . . .
I love to sail forbidden seas."
—HERMAN MELVILLE, *MOBY DICK*

The End . . . or Just the Beginning?

OUR "PALE BLUE DOT," as the legendary planetary scientist Carl Sagan used to call Earth, is small but *mighty*. There may be obstacles ahead, but our planet has survived big messes before, and this 4.5-billion-year-old iron orb, wrapped in rock and water, has shown resilience and awesome staying power.

We have considered seven cosmic catastrophes that could devastate Earth or any one of the billions of other worlds that exist beyond our solar system. But . . . not so fast; there's *us* to consider, too. Today our planet supports upward of 7.3 billion people. Twenty-five years from now, Earth may see 9 billion inhabitants, and the resulting changes to our climate will present many difficult challenges. However, we must recognize the fact that humans have proven to be the most unique group of living creatures to ever set foot on this planet. We possess the ability to shape and change our environments with technologies that can alter and improve upon nature. Whatever is in store for us in the coming years, our "pale blue dot" will likely survive.

There will be more ice ages and asteroid impacts, but we will also experience giant breakthroughs in the fields of bioengineering, genetics, artificial intelligence, cloning, and our destiny-seeking search for other Earth-like planets. We know these changes are inevitable. One of the greatest accomplishments of all will be realized when humans master the ability to sail across seas of stars to build new human civilizations on alien landscapes resembling our own planet Earth. If we do encounter occupants living on these distant worlds, will they consider *us* to be invading aliens?

Now that would be something . . . wouldn't it?

In the Studio with David A. Aguilar

Welcome to Planet Imagination, the
very distant home of my favorite pet alien!

Answering a seemingly simple question can evolve into a highly creative process that produces a new book. I am a very visual thinker; I learn best by decoding illustrations and pictures. This doesn't mean that I don't like the writing process; words can create amazing images, too! Close your eyes and picture these words: "You are standing on a beach. Suddenly the sea rises up and a monstrous 200-foot tidal wave comes thundering in toward you. . . ." Did you see an instant image of that wave in your mind's eye? How can an artist capture such an imagined image? That's the challenge I love most.

Many of my books begin as questions that pop into my head—and my mind is always full of questions! Take this whopper: Is there anything out there that could destroy a planet like Earth? Chasing down a mystery like this can lead me on a very long journey, and let me tell you: galactic answers are often not easy to find!

I live in the Rocky Mountains, not too far from the historic town of Aspen, Colorado. I share my world with raccoons, deer, elk, squirrels, garter snakes, skunks, humming-birds, coyotes, woodpeckers, owls, and red-tailed hawks. Occasionally, a mother bear with young cubs helps my neighbors harvest their apple trees in the fall. At night I look up at the

When I was in school, I made model airplanes, ships, birdhouses—anything I could glue together and paint. All the building skills I developed at a young age I now use to illustrate books like this one. Every time I draw or write I improve these skills.

sky through my telescope. Viewing the planets and stars above my little mountainside home makes me feel close to nature and the universe. The wilderness and vast alpine skies stir my imagination, set many questions in motion, and inspire me to write and create artwork.

I digitally paint on my computer using Photoshop. With this imaging program, the computer screen is my canvas and I "paint" by using my mouse and cursor to manipulate and

layer in digital images; some of those images are photos of models I've made in my art studio. All the images in *Cosmic Catastrophes* were created this way. The artwork in this book is *extremely* complex. Some of it involves as many as sixty separate layers, including small bits and pieces of models digitally combined.

It has taken me years to learn how to perfect this particular process for creating my art. Want to see how I do it? I can show you with an example that's not quite as complicated as the actual art in this book.

I worked with thirty different parts to create this alien artwork that ultimately became the image you see on page 66 in this book.

1. I begin with nothing but a black screen on my computer. This is the background for outer space. A few mouse clicks and I have painted in little white dots for stars.

2. Many, many, *many* clicks later, all the stars are in. Now I click on the Photoshop paintbrush icon, adjust its width, and move my cursor across the screen to create some blue and red gas clouds called nebula. Painting in Photoshop is really just like painting with watercolors . . . but nothing ever spills on your clothes!

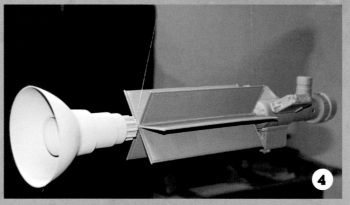

3. To create the giant gas planet on the left, I lightly spray blue and white colors over the starry background with my paintbrush until I've built up a round ball that resembles the planet Neptune. For added interest and depth, I paint in a small moon that looks like it's orbiting the planet. But wouldn't a spaceship be great in this image . . . ?

4. First, I build a model of one out of discarded pieces of plastic found around my house. Look closely and you'll see three printer ink cartridges and a small vitamin bottle at the front of the spaceship; the rear exhaust nozzle is made from a plastic funnel used to pour laundry detergent into a washing machine! I add details by gluing on bits and pieces from an old model tank kit, paint everything a flat white, and hang my spaceship from the ceiling using two pieces of clear fishing line. Next, I photograph it, and voilà! I have an awesome image I can layer into my artwork.

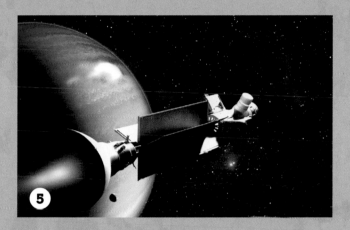 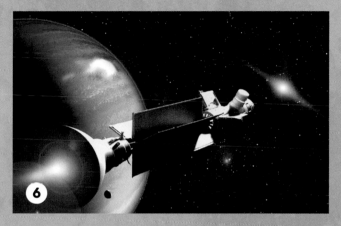

5. Look at that big blast in back! This spaceship is really headed off somewhere! The white I added sets off the exhaust, and the yellow makes the windows glow. The painting is almost finished, but something is still missing: the star that big gas planet orbits.

6. After painting in more rocket exhaust, I use my digital paintbrush to create a sun-like star on the right and add a dust cloud around it where new planets could be forming.

And there you have it: original artwork of a spaceship headed to a new solar system, many, many light years away from Earth. By combining research, homegrown model-making, and painting on a computer, I can make any space vision a reality—even cosmic catastrophes that haven't happened . . . *yet!*

Keep Exploring!

BOOKS

Aguilar, David A. *Alien Worlds: Your Guide to Extraterrestrial Life*. National Geographic, 2013.

——. *Space Encyclopedia: A Tour of Our Solar System and Beyond*. National Geographic, 2013.

——. *Super Stars: The Biggest, Hottest, Brightest, Most Explosive Stars in the Milky Way*. National Geographic, 2010.

——. *13 Planets: The Latest View of the Solar System*. National Geographic, 2011.

Dorling Kindersley. *Space!* DK Smithsonian, 2015.

Simon, Seymour. *Our Solar System*. HarperCollins, 2007.

MEDIA

"Alien Faces," featuring author David A. Aguilar
www.youtube.com/watch?v=qD5dfc_qDP8

"Asteroid Redirect Mission Concept Animation," NASA
www.youtube.com/watch?v=jXvsi7DRyPI

"Killer Asteroids in the Universe," PBS/NOVA
www.youtube.com/watch?v=SQZ7AH09J5w

"National Geographic: Comet Mysteries"
www.youtube.com/watch?v=6Wa4Yme0xuA

WEBSITES

David A. Aguilar author site
www.davidaguilar.org

NASA/Astronomy Picture of the Day (APOD)
http://apod.nasa.gov/apod/astropix.html

NASA/Night Sky Network
http://nightsky.jpl.nasa.gov/

Smithsonian National Air and Space Museum
www.nasm.si.edu

Space.com
www.space.com/science-astronomy/

Index

Note: Page numbers in *italics* refer to illustrations.